WATER

POWER

by Patricia Newman

ENERGY LAB:
WATER POWER

CHERRY LAKE PUBLISHING • ANN ARBOR, MICHIGAN

Published in the United States of America
by Cherry Lake Publishing
Ann Arbor, Michigan
www.cherrylakepublishing.com

Printed in the United States of America
Corporate Graphics Inc.
January 2013
CLFA10

Consultants: Michele Guala, assistant professor in the Department of Civil Engineering and Saint Anthony Falls Laboratory at the University of Minnesota; Marla Conn, reading/literacy specialist and educational consultant

Editorial direction:
Lauren Coss

Book design and illustration:
Emily Love

Photo credits: Shutterstock Images, cover, 1, 5, 7, 11, 18; Library of Congress, 9; Terry Davis/Shutterstock Images, 13; Dmitry Naumov/Shutterstock Images, 15; Jim Parkin/Shutterstock Images, 16; Alex Mit/Shutterstock Images, 21; Bonita R. Cheshier/Shutterstock Images, 23; HO/Finavera Renewables/AP Images, 24; EpicStockMedia/Shutterstock Images, 27

Library of Congress Cataloging-in-Publication Data
Newman, Patricia, 1958-
  Water power / Patricia Newman.
    pages cm. – (Energy Lab)
  Includes bibliographical references and index.
  Audience: 7-8
  Audience: K to grade 3
  ISBN 978-1-61080-899-6 (hardback : alk. paper) – ISBN 978-1-61080-924-5 (paperback : alk. paper) – ISBN 978-1-61080-949-8 (ebook) – ISBN 978-1-61080-974-0 (hosted ebook)
  1. Water-power–Juvenile literature. I. Title.

  TC147.N49 2013
  621.31'2134–dc23

                              2012033416

Cherry Lake Publishing would like to acknowledge the work of The Partnership for 21st Century Skills. Please visit www.21stCenturySkills.org for more information.

TABLE OF CONTENTS

You are being given a mission. The facts in What You Know will help you accomplish it. Remember the clues from What You Know while you are reading the story. The clues and the story will help you answer the questions at the end of the book. Have fun on this adventure!

Water covers more than 70 percent of Earth's surface. People use water for drinking, watering crops, transporting goods, and more. People also use the power of moving water to produce energy. Your mission is to investigate water power as an energy source. What kind of energy does water power give us? How did humans use water power in the past? How do we use water to produce energy today? How might we use water power in the future? Read the facts in What You Know. Then start your mission to learn more about the exciting world of water power!

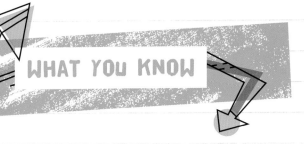

WHAT YOU KNOW

★ More than 80 percent of the energy we produce comes from **fossil fuels** such as oil, coal, and natural gas.

★ Fossil fuels take millions of years to make, and they create greenhouse gases when they are burned.

★ Energy from moving water is clean and **renewable**.

★ We can use rivers, ocean waves, and tides as sources of energy.

Moving water provides clean, renewable energy. We can use this energy to generate power and electricity.

★ Converting water power to electricity does not release extra carbon into the environment.

Sophie York is researching water power for an article she is writing for *Science Kids* magazine. She is conducting research and interviewing experts in the field to learn more about water power as an energy source. Carry out your mission by reading Sophie's Journal.

I'm kicking off my research by visiting my older sister's middle school. Her science teacher, Mr. Donovan, has offered to teach me the basics of water power. He begins by telling me how past cultures have used water power as an energy source.

"Water power may be considered an alternative energy source today," Mr. Donovan begins. "But humans have been harnessing the power of water for longer than you might think! Ancient records are fuzzy, but historians believe the ancient Chinese used water power to grind grain more than 2,000 years ago. Romans were the first to write about water-powered wheels. In the 300s CE, Romans used 16 waterwheels to grind grain in what is now southern France. Waterwheels were an important source of energy throughout Europe from the 1000s on."

Mr. Donovan picks up a small pinwheel from his desk as he talks. "Waterwheels work a lot like this pinwheel I'm holding."

The pinwheel spins as he blows on it.

"Air turns this pinwheel like water turns a waterwheel. The mill uses the energy of motion. This type of energy is called **kinetic energy**. The kinetic energy of the

Years ago, humans captured water power using waterwheels. We harness water power today in different, more efficient ways.

flowing water turns the stones of the waterwheel to grind the grain."

Mr. Donovan explains that people began using hydropower, or power harnessed from water power, to generate electricity in the late 1800s. By 1940, hydropower had become very popular. At that time, it provided 33 percent of U.S. electricity.

THE TENNESSEE VALLEY AUTHORITY

In the 1930s, the United States went through an economic depression. Many people were out of work and living in poverty. In 1933, the U.S. Congress created the Tennessee Valley Authority (TVA). The TVA built dams on the Tennessee River and its tributaries. These dams helped control the floods that often occurred along the river. The dams also generated power that provided badly needed electricity to the region. The new power plants brought many new jobs to the region. Today, the TVA provides power to more than 9 million people in an area covering more than 80,000 square miles (200,000 sq km).

"In the late 1940s, it became cheaper to produce electricity with fossil fuels," Mr. Donovan continues. "Fossil fuels took over as our main source of electricity generation."

Mr. Donovan tells me many people want to make water power a bigger part of our energy production. Burning fossil fuels releases carbon dioxide and other gases into the atmosphere. These gases trap the sun's heat the way heat is trapped in a greenhouse. This is known as the greenhouse effect. The gases are known as greenhouse gases. Many scientists believe the extra heat these gases are trapping

The world's first hydroelectric plant opened in Appleton, Wisconsin, in 1882.

is leading to a gradual warming of Earth's climate. This is known as global warming. That's why water power is such an attractive option. The only greenhouse gases produced when using water power come from the construction of **hydroelectric** facilities and the building of equipment, such as **turbines** and dams. Fossil fuels are still an important part of our energy production, but it's important to keep considering alternative energy sources.

I thank Mr. Donovan for teaching me more about water power. He said that fast-moving water has kinetic energy. I know just the place to capture this energy for electricity. My next stop is a dam. ★

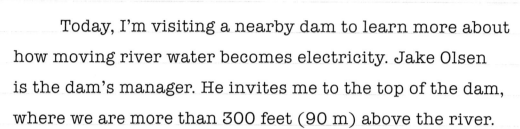

Today, I'm visiting a nearby dam to learn more about how moving river water becomes electricity. Jake Olsen is the dam's manager. He invites me to the top of the dam, where we are more than 300 feet (90 m) above the river.

"Dams are one of the oldest ways to create electricity from moving water," Jake begins. "They have done a lot to provide power and control water across the United States. Dams hold back river water. At first, many dams were built to control floods and water crops. Today, dams are often used to generate hydroelectric power."

THE HOOVER DAM

The Hoover Dam on the Colorado River is one of the most famous dams in the world. It creates so much power that the dam can be maintained using only the money made from power sales. Lake Mead was created when the river was dammed. Like many lakes created by dams, Lake Mead is a reservoir for human use. The lake provides water to Arizona, Nevada, California, and even northern Mexico! People use the lake for fun activities, such as boating.

The Hoover Dam provides water and power to millions of people across the American Southwest.

I peer over the edge of the dam to the river below. "How does the dam produce electricity?" I ask.

Jake smiles. "The dam itself doesn't produce electricity. The dam is a concrete structure that backs up the flow of the river and creates a lake." He points to our left. "Think of the lake as stored energy. When the dam's gates open, water from the lake rushes down a pipe to spin the turbine. The turbine converts the river's kinetic energy to mechanical energy. This mechanical energy runs a **generator**. The generator converts the mechanical energy to electricity. Then the electricity is sent over power lines to your home."

I look at the water tumbling over the dam. "What happens to the water?" I ask.

Jake grins. "That's the best part about water power! The water returns to the river. Unlike fossil fuels, it's a free and renewable fuel source. Hydropower simply borrows the energy in the water before returning it to the river."

I look at the lake on one side of the dam and the river on the other. "You mean this lake wasn't here before the dam?"

"You've got it! The area used to be a river with banks and rocks. It looked a lot like the river on the downstream

Fish ladders help salmon migrate upstream, one step at a time.

side of the dam. The lake flooded everything in its path when the dam was built."

Jake tells me that building the dam changed the natural environment of the riverbed. It destroyed the homes of many animals living along the riverbanks. Fish, such as salmon and steelhead trout, used to migrate upstream to lay their eggs. Now the dam is blocking their path. Fish must climb a special ladder over the dam to swim farther upstream.

I guess there are pros and cons to water power. I wonder if there are ways to use the energy of a moving river without changing the environment. ★

Today I'm about to add another piece to the puzzle. I know that if water is stored in the form of a lake on the upstream side of a dam, electricity can be generated whenever it is needed. But what if the water isn't stored? Can electricity still be generated?

To answer these questions, I've decided to visit another river. Michelle Newman has offered to meet me there. She works for a company that makes electricity from the river's current.

"You picked a great day to stop by, Sophie," Michelle says. "We're actually putting another turbine in the river today." She points to an odd-looking fan. "This is a river turbine. We studied this river very carefully. The size of the turbine's blades is determined by the depth and the speed of the river. The deeper the river, the larger the blades we need."

"Aren't the turbines in the way of ships that travel the river?" I ask. "And what about the fish?"

"Good questions," Michelle says. "We anchor the turbine to the floor of the river. We make sure to place the turbines away from shipping channels. Anything floating on the top of the river floats right over our turbines. Fish and

Rivers are very fast and powerful. We can use the energy rivers produce to generate electricity.

This large turbine is on display at the Glen Canyon Dam in Arizona.

other marine life might get a gentle bump. But the turbines spin too slowly to injure them."

The river is too murky for me to see the bottom. "How many turbines will you put in this river?" I ask.

Michelle smiles at me. "That's a great question! It's actually something we are still trying to figure out. We are currently testing the effects of different numbers of turbines in the water. Placing more turbines does not always mean more electricity. We also need to decide the best spacing for the turbines. If we place them too close together, the turbines interfere with each other. If we place them too far apart, we waste some of the kinetic energy of the river."

Michelle explains some downsides to this type of turbine. She says the dam I visited a few days ago can produce more than 5,000 times as much electricity as one of her turbines. But building dams means changing the river environment. These turbines are much more environmentally friendly.

Wow! I had no idea so much power could come from rivers. I wonder how we use other bodies of water as energy sources. ★

Today I'm visiting another river to study water power. But this river uses tides instead of currents to generate electricity. I'm meeting with Hailey Douglas. She studies tides. I'm hoping she can give me more information about how we use tides to generate power.

Hailey jumps right into the history of tidal power. "More than 1,000 years ago, some people ground grain

A long time ago, humans also used tidal energy to power waterwheels. This old waterwheel worked like turbines do today.

THE PuLL OF THE MOON

As the moon rotates around Earth, it has a gravitational pull on our planet. As it pulls on the nearest oceans, it creates a high tide. On the opposite side of Earth, another high tide occurs. The sun's gravity also tugs at Earth. Its force is weaker than the moon's force because the sun is farther away. About twice a month, during full and new moons, the moon is between the sun and Earth. Together, the sun and the moon tug extra hard at Earth's oceans. This creates tides that are higher than normal.

using waterwheels powered by tides instead of river currents. When the tide flowed in, these devices captured tidal water. This worked a lot like dams holding water. The captured water was released to turn a wheel that moved the grinding stones. Fast-forward to today. Turbines have replaced waterwheels. But the idea is the same."

Hailey tells me that structures called tidal **barrages** capture tidal energy. Tidal barrages are like dams. But instead of harnessing the kinetic energy of a river, they harness the kinetic energy of tides. They work best at the mouth of an **estuary**. Estuaries are places where freshwater mixes with seawater. In an estuary, water flows into a narrow channel. This increases the water's kinetic energy. As the tide rises, the gates of the tidal barrage open. Tidal water flows through the gates and spins the turbines, generating electricity. Then the gates close, holding the water. This works just like a dam. The water rushes out of the barrage when the gates open. It flows back to the ocean, spinning the turbines to generate electricity again.

"Are there any tidal barrages in the United States?" I ask.

"Not yet," Hailey says. "Right now, barrages are only in a few countries, including France, Canada, and China. It's expensive to build a barrage. And the barrage blocks boats and ships that transport goods. But there are other tidal options!"

Hailey explains that tidal energy is very predictable. Two high tides occur every day. But not all places work well for tidal systems. The shape of an area's coastline can change tidal flow and the timing of the tides. The mouth of a river such as this one is where the river opens into the ocean. This happens to be an ideal location for something called tidal stream technology. In tidal stream technology, underwater turbines generate electricity using the tides. The first tidal turbine using tidal stream technology in the United States was placed off the shore of Maine in September 2012.

Ocean turbines are placed on the ocean floor. Their blades capture the kinetic energy from tides and use it to generate power.

Now I'm confused. "What's the difference between your tidal stream technology and the river current turbines I visited yesterday?" I ask.

Hailey grins. "Not too much!" she says. "The turbines you saw yesterday use kinetic energy from the river's current. We use kinetic energy from tides. Otherwise the technology is very similar."

So we use the same basic technology to harness energy from river currents and tides. But tidal energy isn't the only energy we can get from the ocean. I'm off to my last destination! ★

Today I'm at my last stop in my research of water power. I'm meeting with Caleb Maxwell. He works at an experimental energy facility in Oregon. Caleb tells me that Washington, Alaska, Oregon, and Hawaii have the best wave energy potential in the United States. On the West Coast, winds blow from the Pacific Ocean to the shore. The Pacific Ocean is wider than the Atlantic Ocean. Waves have more time to grow as they travel across the Pacific Ocean. This means bigger waves on the West Coast.

HYDROTHERMAL VENTS

Earth's crust is made up of giant plates. Since oceans cover much of Earth's surface, many of these plates meet under water. As the plates shift, small cracks form. Seawater trickles through the cracks to Earth's core of hot magma. The seawater becomes super-heated to 700 degrees Fahrenheit (370°C) and returns through hydrothermal vents that are 7,500 feet (2,300 m) deep. The extreme pressure at these depths prevents the water from boiling. If we can channel the energy of hydrothermal vents to the surface, these vents might become the next source of renewable water power.

Taller, longer, and faster waves mean more energy. Huge waves, such as this one off the coast of Kauai, Hawaii, carry a lot of energy.

"Wave energy is still being studied," Caleb says. "But it could be a terrific contribution to our nation's renewable energy. Especially here on the West Coast."

"What about Alaska and Hawaii?" I ask.

"Those states have excellent wave potential too. But they are far from the other 48 states. Electricity generated by wave technologies would stay in those states. Energy from the West Coast could be used across the country."

Something Caleb said confuses me. "What are wave technologies?" I ask.

"There are several technologies we use to extract energy from waves." He explains as he pulls out a chart from his backpack. "One type is point absorbers. These are buoys that float on the water but are attached to the ocean floor. The kinetic energy of the yellow buoys bobbing on the waves becomes electrical energy. Each buoy generates enough electricity to power 24,900 homes."

This point absorber buoy sits on top of the ocean water. Waves from the ocean power a turbine inside to produce electricity.

I look out over the Pacific Ocean. It's hard to imagine that the waves I'm seeing could produce so much power.

"Another kind of technology is called an overtopping device," Caleb continues. He points to the second drawing on the chart. "Waves lift water over a barrier and fill a reservoir. The water in the reservoir drains through a turbine. The turbine generates electricity."

Caleb shows me one last picture. This technology looks like an upside-down pendulum. "Let me guess what this one does," I say. "The upside-down pendulum moves with the back-and-forth motion of the waves."

Caleb nods. "We call that motion surge."

"Okay. The waves surge and force the lever back and forth. The lever is connected to a motor. The motor turns kinetic energy into mechanical energy. Then a generator turns the mechanical energy into electricity."

Caleb smiles. "Yes, and there are even more ways we can turn wave energy into electricity. Scientists are working hard to perfect these technologies and come up with new ones."

Wow! I can't wait to see how we use water power in the future! ★

Nice work! You've learned a lot about water power as an energy source. We can use the moving water from rivers and oceans to produce energy. You understand that dams can provide a lot of electricity. But they change the environment. River turbines and tidal turbines don't change the environment very much. But they don't produce nearly enough power on their own to meet our energy needs. You also learned about new wave technologies. While these don't play a large role in our water power use right now, they may be an important part of our energy future. Scientists and engineers keep exploring new and better ways to use water power. Congratulations on completing your mission!

CONSIDER THIS

★ Describe how water flows through a dam to generate electricity.

★ Explain how a tidal barrage works.

Water power is used in different ways all over the world. How is water power being used to create electricity near your town?

★ How do hydrothermal vents differ from other forms of ocean energy?

★ Find out if water power is being used to generate electricity in your town. Describe which method is used—for example, a dam, tidal turbines, wave energy, or another option.

★ Which water power technology discussed in Sophie's journal do you think is most promising? Why?

barrage (BAHR-ij) a low dam built across an estuary to capture energy produced by tides

estuary (ES-choo-er-ee) a body of water formed by freshwater rivers and streams emptying into the saltwater of the ocean

fossil fuel (FAH-suhl fyoo-uhl) coal, oil, or natural gas formed from ancient plants and animals

generator (JEN-uh-ray-tur) a machine that produces electricity

hydroelectric (hye-droh-i-LEK-trik) generating electricity from flowing water

kinetic energy (ki-net-ik EN-ur-jee) the energy of motion

renewable (ri-NOO-uh-buhl) when something can never be used up

reservoir (REZ-ur-vwahr) a place where something collects

tributary (TRIB-yuh-ter-ee) a stream or branch of a river that feeds into a larger river

turbine (TUR-buhn) a machine that spins an electric generator

BOOKS

Benduhn, Tea. *Water Power*. Pleasantville, NY: Weekly
    Reader, 2009.

Burgan, Michael. *Water Power*. New York: Chelsea
    Clubhouse, 2010.

Spilsbury, Richard. *Water, Wave, and Tidal Power*.
    New York: PowerKids Press, 2012.

WEB SITES

Alliant Energy Kids

http://www.alliantenergykids.com/
EnergyandTheEnvironment/RenewableEnergy/022399

    Learn more about the history of water power.

Energy Kids

http://www.eia.gov/kids/energy.cfm?page=hydropower_
home-basics

    Learn more about the many sources of water power
    described in this book.

Energy Quest

http://energyquest.ca.gov/index.html

    This site contains tons of great information on energy,
    including a story, movies, and more.

BUILD YOUR OWN TURBINE

You will need an empty half-gallon cardboard milk carton. With an adult's help, use a nail to punch one hole in the exact middle of the top of the carton. Punch two additional holes in the bottom right corner and the bottom left corner. Put heavy tape over these two holes. Fill the carton with water. Hang the carton from a tree outside. Rip the tape off one corner. What happens? Rip the tape off the other corner. What happens? Explain what is happening with the concepts you learned in this book.

HOW DO YOU USE ENERGY?

Draw a map of your home. Visit each room to find the items that use energy, such as lights, the thermostat to regulate heat or air-conditioning, televisions, computers, appliances, and so on. Indicate whether these items were on or off when you visited each room. Ask your parents what types of energy your home uses, such as solar power or natural gas. Can you think of ways to conserve energy in your home?

INDEX

Patricia Newman is the author of several books for children, including *Jingle the Brass*, a Junior Library Guild Selection and a Smithsonian-recommended book, and *Nugget on the Flight Deck*, a California Reading Association Eureka! Silver Honor Book for Nonfiction.

ABOUT THE CONSULTANTS

Michele Guala has always been fascinated by the motion of water in natural environments. He works by the Mississippi River and lives in Minneapolis, Minnesota, with his wife and his son.

Marla Conn is a reading/literacy specialist and an educational consultant. Her specialized consulting work consists of assigning guided reading levels to trade books, writing and developing user guides and lesson plans, and correlating books to curriculum and national standards.